George Newbold Lawrence

Descriptions of New Species of Birds from Mexico, Central America and South America

With a note on Ralus longirostris

George Newbold Lawrence

Descriptions of New Species of Birds from Mexico, Central America and South America
With a note on Ralus longirostris

ISBN/EAN: 9783337315313

Printed in Europe, USA, Canada, Australia, Japan

Cover: Foto ©Andreas Hilbeck / pixelio.de

More available books at **www.hansebooks.com**

ANNALS

OF THE

LYCEUM OF NATURAL HISTORY.

I.—*Descriptions of New Species of Birds from Mexico, Central America, and South America, with a Note on Rallus longirostris.*

BY GEO. N. LAWRENCE.

Read January 30th, 1871.

Some of the birds described in this paper were obtained by the late Col. A. J. Grayson, of Mazatlan, most of them on the Island of Socorro, off the Pacific coast of Mexico. Col. Grayson's collection, with others made in Northwestern Mexico, were kindly placed in my hands by Prof. Henry, of the Smithsonian Institution, for examination, with a view to furnishing a catalogue of them, in which the notes of Col. Grayson are to be incorporated. As some time will elapse before this can be prepared and published, I have thought best, preliminary to its appearance, to describe the new species.

Several of the species have MS. names given them by Prof. Baird, which in all such cases have been retained.

1. Harporhynchus graysoni, Baird, MS.

Male. Above of a rather dull reddish-brown, the front paler, a blackish spot in front of and under the eye; chin, upper part of throat and sides of the head pale ochreous, the latter marked with narrow faint dusky bars; tail dark liver-brown, the outer three feathers with a grayish spot on the inner web at the end; quills of the same color as the tail, the larger ones narrowly edged with dull white, the others with dull pale rufous; the entire under-plumage is pale yellowish fulvous, sides darker, with longitudinal brown stripes; bill black; tarsi and toes blackish-brown.

Length (fresh) $11\frac{1}{2}$ in.; wing $4\frac{1}{4}$; tail $5\frac{1}{4}$; bill $\frac{3}{4}$; tarsi $1\frac{3}{8}$.

Habitat. Socorro Island, Mexico. Collected by Col. A. J. Grayson, June, 1865. Type in Museum of the Smithsonian Institution, No. 59987.

The female (No. 50808) differs in being brownish on the under-plumage, without any of the yellowish tint.

Remarks. This is so distinct from all others of the genus, that no comparisons are required.

Note by Col. Grayson.

"*Socorro Thrush, Mocking-Bird.* Iris brown; bill and feet black, nails do.; soles of feet dull yellow. First primary very short or spurious, third and fourth longest; tails lightly forked when closed.

"Not very abundant, but seems to be well distributed over the island. It has all the characteristics of the true Mocking-Bird (*Mimus polyglottus*) in its habits. Of solitary disposition, it attacks every bird of its own species that approaches its usual haunts. There was one that took up its quarters in our camp, and was certainly the tamest bird of this genus I ever saw. He appeared to take pleasure in our society, and attacked furiously every bird that came near us; he doubtless regarded us as his own property, often perching upon the table when we were taking our meals, and eating from our hands, as though he had been brought up to this kind of treatment; at times ascending to the branches over our heads, he would break forth into loud and mellow song, very thrush-like. In the still hours of the night, while roosting on the branches near us, he would sometimes utter a few dreamy notes, recalling to mind the well-known habits of the true Mocking-Bird."

2. Cistothorus æquatorialis.

Male. Upper plumage brownish rufous, brightest on the rump; the feathers of the crown and hind neck have their centres marked with paler, nearly obsolete stripes; a stripe of pale rufous extends from over the eye to the hind neck, sides of the head and neck clear light rufous; a narrow dark brown line runs from the angle of the mouth under the eye; the interscapular feathers are blackish-brown, with conspicuous shaft stripes of pale fulvous; tail light rufous, with transverse narrow bars of black, on the central feathers there are thirteen bars, on the others they are broader and wider apart; quills dark umber-brown, the outer primaries narrowly margined with white, the outer webs of the smaller quills and the wing coverts are light rufous, more or less transversely marked with blackish-brown; the under surface is pale rufous, whitish on the throat and middle of the abdomen, brighter on the flanks and under tail coverts; under wing coverts whitish; upper mandible light-brown, the under pale yellowish-white, dusky at the tip; tarsi and toes yellowish-white.

Length (skin) about $4\frac{1}{2}$ in.; wing $1\frac{3}{4}$; tail $1\frac{5}{8}$; bill $\frac{7}{16}$; tarsi $\frac{3}{4}$.

Habitat. Pichincha, Ecuador. Type in the Museum of Vassar College, from the collection of Prof. J. Orton.

Remarks. This species seems of a somewhat stouter form than *C. stellaris*, with longer tarsi and bill; the colors are lighter and more rufous; it may be distinguished by the absence of dark brown on the crown, and its clear rufous uropygium; the tail also is rufous, with narrower and more numerous bands.

3. Troglodytes insularis, Baird, MS.

Male. Plumage above of a dull light brown, slightly rufescent, and crossed with narrow faint dusky bars, front paler, the feathers of the crown have lighter margins; the concealed feathers of the rump end with white; lores, a narrow line over the eye, sides of the head, and the entire under-plumage of a clear pale fulvous, the under-tail coverts with dusky bars; tail light brown, crossed with numerous dark brown bars, on the outer feathers the interspaces are whitish; the primary and secondary quills have their inner webs dark liver-brown, the outer webs are light brown with whitish indentations, tertiaries light brown, barred with darker brown; upper mandible brown, the under yellowish-white, dusky at the end; tarsi and toes yellowish-brown.

Length (fresh) 5 in.; wing $1\frac{7}{8}$; tail $1\frac{3}{4}$; bill $\frac{3}{8}$; tarsi $\frac{3}{4}$.

Habitat. Socorro Island, Mexico. Collected by Col. A. J. Grayson. Type in Mus. Smithsonian Institution, No. 50810.

Remarks. This somewhat resembles *T. inquietus* from Panama, but that species has a stouter bill, the colors are more rufous, and the bars more clearly defined; the flanks and undertail coverts are of a darker rufous, the former faintly barred, the latter with dark brown bars and ending with white.

Note by Col. Grayson.

"*Socorro Wren.* Iris brown; bill dark brown above, under mandible paler; feet brown, nails black; wings much rounded, the fifth and sixth primaries longest.

"This busy little wren is the most common bird I met with upon the Island, and everywhere its cheerful song may be heard in the trees, or among the brambles and rocks; like all the birds peculiar to this Island, it is very tame. I often saw it feeding upon dead land-crabs; and I may here remark, that all the birds inhabiting the Island, with the exception of doves and parrots, subsist more or less upon this crustacean."

4. **Parula insularis.**

Male. Plumage above of a clear bluish-gray, a patch of dull greenish-yellow in the middle of the back; a blackish mark surrounds the fore part of the eye; tail feathers brownish-black, with margins the color of the back, the outer two feathers on each side have a small spot of dull white on the inner web near the end; the smaller wing coverts and exposed portions of the others, and of the inner quills, are the color of the back; the concealed parts of the middle and larger coverts are black, the ends of both largely marked with white; the quills are blackish-brown, the outer with narrow whitish edges; inside of wings white; under-plumage bright yellow, deepening to orange on the upper breast and on the flanks, lower part of abdomen light fulvous, in the middle and on the under tail coverts creamy-white, thighs light ashy brown; upper mandible black, the under yellow, with the tip brown; tarsi and toes brown.

Length (skin) $4\frac{1}{2}$ in.; wing $2\frac{1}{8}$; tail $1\frac{7}{8}$; bill $\frac{7}{16}$; tarsi $\frac{3}{4}$.

Habitat. Tres Marias Islands, Mexico. Collected by Col. A. J. Grayson. Type in Mus. Smithsonian Institution, No. 50796. Four specimens in the collection are all males.

In the collection made by Col. Grayson at Socorro Island, are eight specimens of *Parula*, only one of which has the sex indicated, viz., No. 50804, a female; they are probably the same as the males from the Tres Marias; they differ in having the upper plumage more gray, scarcely showing any shading of blue, but with the rump tinged with greenish-yellow, and the quills and tail feathers edged with the same color; below they are of a paler yellow; all the Socorro Island birds are much alike, which may be due to seasonal change, as it is not probable that all the specimens are females.

Remarks. Col. Grayson says of this species, "perhaps *Parula pitiayumi*," but they are very distinct. That species is of a deeper and more decided blue above than all others of the genus, whereas the present bird is paler. *P. pitiayumi* is entirely of a deep yellow below, with the lores a decided black; in the present species the lower part of the abdomen is whitish and the lores dusky; it also has the tail longer and the wings shorter than those of *P. pitiayumi*.

Note by Col. Grayson.

"Iris brown; bill black above, dull yellow below towards the base and black at tip; feet brown, with yellow soles, claws dark brown; indistinct shady bars across the upper part of tail feathers. This bird seems to be identical with the Tres Marias species, and is quite common on the Socorro; it is a little larger than the Marias' bird, and less white at the extremities of the tail feathers."

5. Hæmophila sumichrasti.

Female. The feathers of the back are pale rufous, broadly marked down their centres with dark brown, the rump is immaculate and the upper tail coverts bright rufous; the feathers of the crown have dark brown shaft-stripes, with their edges brighter rufous than those of the back, there is a narrow cinereous stripe from the bill over the centre of the crown to the hind neck; a broader stripe of ashy-white extends from the bill over the eye, along each side of the crown as far back as the central stripe; below, and bordering this, is a brownish-red postocular stripe, also one from the bill to the eye; sides of the head and of the neck, lower part of the throat and the breast, of a pale ashy color, upper part of throat and abdomen grayish-white, the latter washed with very pale rufous, flanks and under tail coverts light rufous; a short, narrow brown line extends back from the angle of the mouth, and another parallel to it down the side of the chin on each side; the two central tail feathers are of a rather bright rufous, and are crossed with dusky, nearly obsolete bars, the other tail feathers have their inner webs brownish-rufous, the outer webs colored like the central feathers, the outer feather very pale rufous; quills liver-brown, margined with dull pale rufous, smaller wing coverts deep bright rufous, the middle and greater coverts blackish-brown edged with very pale rufous; "iris brownish-red; upper mandible brown, the lower mandible and feet fleshy."

Length (skin) $5\frac{5}{8}$ in.; wing $2\frac{1}{2}$; tail $2\frac{5}{8}$; tarsi $\frac{3}{4}$.

Habitat. Tuchitan, Tehuantepec, Mexico. Collected by Prof. F. Sumichrast, September 8, 1868. Type in Mus. Smithsonian Institution, No. 54139.

Remarks. With the exception of the very different markings about the head, this species in coloring much resembles my *H. melanotis;* but it is much smaller, and differs from it in there being no black on the crown or sides of the head, and in having two narrow stripes extending downwards from the bill, on each side of the throat.

I found a single specimen of this species in a remarkably fine collection of birds made by Prof. F. Sumichrast, in Southwestern Mexico, belonging to the Smithsonian Institution, and submitted to me for examination by Prof. Henry. It contains many species of much interest, but so far this is the only one I feel satisfied to describe as new.

Since my determination of it as a new species, I have received a letter from Prof. Sumichrast, containing a full description and an accurate drawing of the head, apparently of the same bird, which he writes he is tempted to consider new. It is, therefore, with much pleasure I dedicate it to him.

6. Pipilo carmani.

Male. Whole upper plumage, head, throat, and upper part of the breast olivaceous brown, with a reddish cast; there is a spot of white on the centre of the throat (this last character varies in size in different individuals); tail blackish-brown, edged with olivaceous and crossed with almost obsolete dusky bars, the outer two feathers on each side with an irregular oval spot of white on their inner webs at the end; quills dark hair-brown, with grayish margins; the wing coverts blackish-brown, the greater and middle coverts, the scapulars and the tertiaries spotted with white at their ends; lower part of breast and middle of abdomen white, sides broadly marked with bright ferruginous, the under tail coverts pale ferruginous; upper mandible brownish-black, the under paler; tarsi and toes light fleshy-brown.

Length 6½ in.; wing 2¾; tail 3; bill ½; tarsi 1

The female differs only in having the color of the upper plumage and that of the throat of a lighter brown; the coloring of the abdomen, and the sides are the same in both sexes.

Habitat. Socorro Island, Mexico. Collected by Col. A. J. Grayson, June, 1865. Types in Mus. Smithsonian Institution, No. 50843, No. 39990.

Remarks. As will be seen, this is quite a diminutive species; its style of coloring is like that of *P. erythropthalmus, P.*

arcticus, &c. It may readily be known from all others by its smaller size.

Col. Grayson requested that this species might be named after his friend, Dr. B. F. Carman, of Mazatlan, to whom he was under many obligations. With this request it gratifies me to be able to comply.

Note by Col. Grayson.

"Iris reddish-hazel; bill black; tarsi and toes brown; nails brown.

"This is an abundant species, found in all the thickets of the Island; many of them took up their abode in our camp, picking up crumbs about our feet, as tame as domestic fowls. They delighted in bathing in the water we had placed in a basin on the ground for their use, and frequent combats took place between them for this privilege. It was through the agency of this species that water was discovered in a locality where we had not the remotest idea of finding it, and for this providential service he was a welcome visitor and a privileged character."

7. **Attila cinnamomeus.**

Male. Upper plumage of a rather light reddish cinnamon, the rump and upper tail coverts pale yellowish-cinnamon, the coverts lightest in color; front, superciliary stripe and sides of the head clear light yellow, all the feathers having black shaft-stripes; the throat and breast are clear yellow, the centres of the feathers with dusky flammulations, abdomen and under tail coverts bright lemon-yellow, sides of the breast and flanks bright pale cinnamon, thighs yellow, tinged with cinnamon; tail clear cinnamon, of a brighter color than the back; quills dark brown, the primaries edged with grayish, the secondaries with light cinnamon; the smaller wing coverts are the color of the back, the middle and larger are blackish-brown ending with cinnamon; under wing coverts bright yellow, axillaries tinged with cinnamon; bill brownish horn-color, both mandibles whitish at tip, the hook much elongated; tarsi and toes brown.

Length (skin) $8\frac{1}{2}$ in.; wing $3\frac{7}{8}$; tail $3\frac{1}{2}$; bill 1; tarsi 1.

The female differs in having grayish-white on the front, sides of the head, throat and breast, in place of the yellow of the male; the abdomen is creamy-white, with a slight tinge of yellow on the lower part; under tail coverts very pale yellow; under wing coverts light yellow.

Habitat. Mazatlan, Mexico. Collected by Col. A. J. Grayson. Types in Museum of Smithsonian Institute, ♂ No. 58231; ♀ No. 58232.

Remarks. Three specimens are in Col. Grayson's collection, two marked *A. sclateri* and one *A. citreopygius*, but I think it a very distinct species from both; its affinities are with *A. citreopygius*, from which it differs in its upper plumage being not at all tinged with brown, the light marking on the rump apparently more restricted, the yellow coloring below clearer and brighter, without any brown on the sides of the breast, and the under wing coverts yellow—not light cinnamon as in that species; the tail is lighter in color, not inclining to brown; the feathers overlying the pleura are brighter in color and more elongated; it is larger than *A. citreopygius*, the tail being half an inch more in length than that of the other; the bill is more slender, with the hook conspicuously longer, and much lighter in color. *A. sclateri* has not been found, I think, north of Costa Rica; it may be distinguished by the olive-green which prevails in its upper plumage, also on the neck and breast.

8. Todirostrum superciliaris.

Crown and hind neck dark grayish-plumbeous, the front blackish; a white stripe extends from over the eye quite forward on the bill; lores blackish; back and rump bright olive-green; tail black, margined with olive-green; wing coverts black, the ends broadly marked with bright yellow; quills brownish-black, edged with bright yellow; under wing coverts yellow; the under-plumage is pearly-white, with the upper part of the breast light plumbeous; a wash of pale yellow on the lower part of the abdomen and under tail coverts; sides under the wings light olive-green; bill black, whitish at the end; tarsi and toes pale brown.

Length $3\frac{7}{8}$ in.; wing 2; tail $1\frac{3}{8}$; tarsi $\frac{3}{4}$; bill $\frac{1}{2}$.

Habitat. Venezuela? Collected by Mr. Christopher Wood, of Philadelphia. Type in my collection.

Remarks. In general appearance this comes nearest to *T. schistaceiceps*, Scl., but has the crown of a lighter shade; is much whiter below, the ashy coloring occupying only a small space on the upper part of the breast; the yellow markings on the wings are much broader and brighter; the wings, tarsi and tail are longer; a very distinguishing character is the white stripe, which runs from over the eye to the nostrils, on each side of the crown, whereas *T. schistaceiceps* has a white spot in front of the eye, not extending over it.

9. Elainea macilvainii.

Upper plumage greenish-olive, yellowish-green on the rump; front and crown blackish-brown, with a crest of light sulphur-yellow; a line from the bill over the eye and circle round the eye grayish-white; lores dusky; tail light umber-brown, edged with yellowish-green; the smaller wing coverts are colored like the back, the other coverts are dark brown, the middle ones ending with very pale yellow, forming a transverse band, and the larger edged with the same color; quills blackish-brown, the primaries narrowly and the secondaries rather broadly margined with pale yellow; under wing coverts light yellow; chin and throat grayish-white, sides of the breast dusky olive-green, middle of the breast pale yellow, the feathers with ashy centres, the abdomen and under tail coverts are of a clear, rather pale yellow; bill and feet black.

Length $4\frac{3}{4}$ in.; wing $2\frac{1}{4}$; tail $2\frac{1}{8}$; tarsi $\frac{5}{8}$; bill $\frac{3}{8}$.

Habitat. Venezuela? Collected by Mr. Christopher Wood. Type in my collection.

Remarks. This fly-catcher in coloring most resembles *E. placens*, Scl., but is much smaller, with the upper plumage of a darker shade; the wings and tail each measure half an inch less than those of that species; the top of the head is darker and the crest much paler; by these differences it is easily distinguished.

I have named this species in compliment to my friend, J. H. McIlvain, Esq., of Philadelphia, an ethnologist as well as ornithologist, to whose liberality Mr. Wood is indebted for the opportunity to make the collection, from which I obtained this and the preceding species.

Unfortunately, Mr. Wood lost a considerable portion of his collection by shipwreck.

10. Empidonax fulvipectus.

Male. The entire upper plumage is brownish-olive, the crown and lengthened crest are a little darker; lores dusky gray; a conspicuous circle of pale yellow around the eye; tail dark brown, the outer web of the outside feather dull white, the other feathers edged with olive; the smaller wing coverts are the color of the back, the middle and larger are blackish-brown, ending with dull pale fulvous, forming two bars across the wing; quills blackish-brown, with olive-green margins; under wing coverts pale tawny yellow; under plumage dull yellow, the chin grayish, the breast and upper part of the abdomen of an olivaceous brownish-fulvous, middle of abdomen light buffy yellow; the upper mandible is brownish-black, the under pale yellow; tarsi and toes brownish-black.

Length $5\frac{2}{3}$ in.; wing 3; tail $2\frac{3}{4}$; bill $\frac{7}{16}$; tarsi $\frac{5}{8}$.

The bill is very narrow and tapers regularly from the base, not the least bulging at the sides; the third quill is the longest, second and fourth nearly as long, first and sixth equal.

Habitat. City of Mexico. Type in my collection.

Remarks. This species in its peculiar coloring is somewhat like *E. bairdii*, Scl., but may readily be known by its more slender form, longer wings and tail, its general duller color, decided brownish breast, and slender bill, this last in *E. bairdii* being quite broad.

The bill exceeds in length that of *E. hammondi*, while it is quite as narrow at the base.

11. Trogon eximius.

Trogon viridis, Lawr., Ann. Lyc. N. Y., Vol. vii., p. 290.

Male. Crown and hind neck dark violet-blue, back of a shining dark green, more or less mixed with violet-blue, rump and upper tail coverts deep violet-blue; front, cheeks, chin, and throat black; breast fine violet-blue, connecting with the same color on the hind neck; abdomen and under tail coverts very deep orange, sides dark grayish slate-color, thighs sooty black; two middle tail feathers green, with a decided wash of blue, the outer webs of the next two feathers are of the same color, the inner webs black—the ends of all these end narrowly with black, the outer three feathers are white, their concealed bases being black; wings black; the quill feathers have their bases white, the primaries are narrowly edged with white for two-thirds their length; the upper mandible is whitish horn-color, with the base pale plumbeous, the under is dark plumbeous; feet dark brown, the soles yellow.

Mr. J. Galbraith, in his note of this species, says, "very common, light blue about the eyes, irides brown."

Length (fresh) $10\frac{1}{2}$ in.; wing $5\frac{3}{8}$; tail 6; tarsi $\frac{1}{2}$.

The female is of a plumbeous slate-color, grayish on the breast, the abdomen and under tail coverts orange; primaries of a rich dark brown; the wing coverts and smaller quills are black, crossed with very narrow undulating white lines, rather widely separated; tail blackish-brown, with a purplish gloss, the three lateral feathers are white at their ends, the outer web of the outer feather is barred with white, and has a few irregular bars of the same color on the inner web, both webs of the next feather also have a few white bars.

Habitat. Isthmus of Panama. Types in my collection.

Remarks. In my catalogue of birds from Panama, I included this species as *T. viridis*, Linn.; but as it differs so materially from that species, I consider it to be distinct.

In general coloration it somewhat resembles *T. viridis*, but is rather smaller; the back is mixed with violet-blue, and the rump is of a more intense violet-blue color; the wash of blue on the tail is more apparent, and the orange of the under parts is of a deeper shade; but the most distinguishing character is that of the outer tail feathers, which have a much greater extent of white on their terminal portions, when the tail is closed, the under side appears entirely white, the black bases being quite concealed, whereas in *T. viridis* the ends of the feathers only are white, the black basal portions showing conspicuously.

Specimens referred to *T. venustus*, Cab., by Mr. Cassin, are in Prof. Orton's collection, from Archidona, Ecuador; they agree quite well with Cabanis' description, except in being of the same size as *T. viridis*, not "somewhat smaller," and that the abdomen is deep orange; he says, "belly yellowish-orange;" in describing *T. viridis*, he has, "belly orange," but this is perhaps a variable character.

Compared with examples of *T. viridis* from Bahia, Prof. Orton's specimens are more of an azure instead of violet-blue, the upper plumage more golden, the rump less violet, being mixed with green; the middle tail feathers are green, without any shading of blue, and the abdomen and under tail coverts of a deeper orange; in the extent of white on the end of the tail feathers, they agree with *T. viridis*.

These comparative differences with *T. viridis* are very similar to those pointed out by Dr. Cabanis; as he makes no allusion to the ending of the outer tail feathers, I infer they are the same in both.

Specimens exactly corresponding with those from Archidona are in collections received by Prof. Orton from Mr. J. Hauxwell, at Pebas on the Upper Amazon; also, I have an example from Bogota.

The new species differs from the specimens above spoken of as *T. venustus*, in the head and breast being of a deeper blue, the rump intensely violet instead of greenish; the middle tail feathers, instead of being green, are more blue even than those of *T. viridis;* the greater extent of white on the outer tail feathers distinguishes it from this as well as from *T. viridis;* the orange coloring below is of a deeper color than in either *T. venustus* or *T. viridis*.

12. **Chlorostilbon caribæus.**

Male. Crown of a glittering pale golden-green, upper plumage and wing coverts grass-green, somewhat golden; the entire under-plumage is of a brilliant uniform emerald-green, with a few white feathers on the flanks; tail steel-blue; wings brownish-purple; bill black; feet dark brown.

Length about $3\frac{1}{4}$ in.; wing $1\frac{3}{4}$; tail $1\frac{1}{8}$; bill $\frac{5}{8}$.

Habitat. Island of Curaçao. Type in my collection.

Remarks. Its nearest ally appears to be *C. atala*, but that species is entirely of a golden-green; the new species is only slightly golden above, not the least so in its under-plumage, where it is of a much darker shade of green, and more glittering; the tail is strikingly larger and the feathers broader, the color of which is more blue, that of *C. atala* being more of a steel-black; the wings are longer, and the bill appears to be stouter than in that species.

Three specimens were presented to me by my friend, Mr. T. Bland; he obtained them from Mr. Henry H. Raven, who brought them from the Island of Curaçao. Two of the specimens are immature males.

13. Conurus holochlorus var. brevipes, Baird, M. S.

Male. The general plumage is grass-green; the abdomen is lighter and has a yellowish cast; ends and inner margins of quills blackish; inside of quills and under-surface of the tail dull yellowish; bill yellowish-white; feet light yellow.

There is no difference in the plumage of the sexes.

Length (fresh) $12\frac{1}{4}$ in.; wing $6\frac{3}{4}$; tail $6\frac{1}{2}$; tarsi $\frac{5}{8}$.

Habitat. Socorro Island, Mexico. Collected by Col. A. J. Grayson, "Spring of 1865." Type in Mus. Smithsonian Institution, No. 39971.

Remarks. Six specimens before me, compared with two examples of *C. holochlorus* from Salvador, have the toes uniformly shorter; the wings of the Socorro Island bird are half an inch shorter than in those from Salvador; in plumage there is no perceptible difference in the two forms.

Mexico, Central America, and South America. 15

The toes of the two forms measure as follows:—
C. *holochlorus*—Outer toe $\frac{15}{16}$; middle $1\frac{1}{8}$; inner $\frac{3}{4}$; hind $\frac{1}{2}$.
C. *brevipes*—   " $\frac{3}{4}$;   " $\frac{7}{8}$;   " $\frac{5}{8}$;   " $\frac{3}{8}$.

Note by Col. Grayson.

"*Socorro Parrot.* Iris reddish-brown; bill yellowish-white, dark or black at point; feet pale yellow, with brownish scutellæ; nails dark brown. Contents of the stomach, kernels of nuts.

" This Parakeet is quite abundant and evidently belonging to this locality, which it never leaves; they are to be met with in flocks or in pairs. In the mornings they left the cove in which we were encamped, for the higher regions of the interior, to feed, returning again in the evening to roost; this cove, in which the trees are larger and the shade more dense than in other parts of the Island, seems to be their favorite resort. I saw them at times walking about on the ground beneath these trees, apparently picking up clay or gravel. They are remarkably tame, exhibiting no fear in our presence; three cages were soon filled with them, which were caught by hand, and their constant whistling for their mates brought many of them into camp, perching upon the cages and elsewhere. They feed upon a hard nut which they find in the mountain-gorges, and on account of the inaccessible localities where this fruit grew, I was unable to find it; the powerful jaws of this Parakeet would indicate the fruit to be very hard."

14. Leptoptila bonapartii.

Male. Above of a light brownish-olive, a little browner on the wings and more olivaceous on the lower back and upper tail coverts, hind neck grayish, with a bluish tinge; front whitish, with a slight roseate tint, crown plumbeous-blue, grayish on the forward part and darker towards the occiput; throat white, sides of the head light brownish-vinaceous, this color extending somewhat on the hind neck; breast and upper part of abdomen of a pale roseate color, lower part of abdomen and under tail coverts white, sides under the wings light cinnamon-brown; four middle tail feathers colored like the back, the others purplish-black, terminating in white; under wing coverts dark bright cinnamon; the inner webs of the primaries light cinnamon, the larger quills are of a fine dark brown, the exposed portions of the others colored like the back; bill black; feet yellow.

Length $10\frac{1}{2}$ in.; wing $5\frac{3}{4}$; tail 4; bill $1\frac{1}{10}$; tarsi $1\frac{3}{10}$.

Habitat. Mexico (A. Sallé). Type in Mus. Smithsonian Institution, No. 29693.

Remarks. This specimen was received from Mr. Sallé and labelled by him "*L. albifrons*, Bp.;" the reverse side of the lable is marked " ♂ P. V. Juin, '59." It no doubt was supervised by Bonaparte, as Sallé's birds mostly were; it is very distinct from the species, which is now admitted to be entitled to bear that name, viz., the bird for some time known as *L. brachyptera*, Gray.

I found this specimen in the collection of the Smithsonian Institution (where there are numerous specimens of the true *L. albifrons*) about two years ago, and hesitated to describe it as new, fearing to add to the confusion attached to the name of *albifrons*. In general coloration it somewhat resembles that species, which differs in being of a lighter olive above and more roseate on the breast, it has a much longer tail, with no plumbeous on the crown, and may be known from all its allies by the inner webs of the primaries being just edged with pale cinnamon.

L. plumbeiceps, Scl. & Salv. (P. Z. S., 1868, p. 59), differs in being dark brown above, in having the plumage of the breast somewhat darker, and the under-lining of the wings of a more intense color; in the new bird the plumbeous is confined to the crown, and does not extend on the hind neck, as in *L. plumbeiceps*.

It really comes nearest to *L. rufaxilla*, from South America, in general coloration, but that species has the breast more roseate, the blue of the head lighter and more restricted, the sides of the head cinnamon color, and the feet smaller.

Under the circumstances I consider the name conferred a very appropriate one.

15. Zenaidura graysoni, Baird, M. S.

Male. Entire plumage above olivaceous-brown, with a rufescent tinge, the crown of a darker brown; front, sides of the head, and the whole under-plumage dark cinnamon red, except the chin, which is paler; auricular spot black, but not very distinct; the sides under the wings grayish-plumbeous; the two central tail feathers are of the same color as the back, with their centres blackish-plumbeous; the next feather on each side has the outer web and end colored like the back, with a rather indistinct subterminal black bar on the inner web, below which the inner web is dark plumbeous, the next pair on each side are grayish-plumbeous, the outer webs broadly margined and tipped with brown, and having the subterminal black bar more distinct, the next two on each side of a light plumbeous-gray, just margined with brown on the outer webs, and with the black bars still darker, the outer feather has its end and the outer web pale bluish-white, the inner web dark plumbeous, the black spot mostly confined to the inner web; the tail feathers underneath are brownish-black, except the outer web of the lateral one, the end of which and those of the next two are light plumbeous, the ends of the others becoming darker towards the central ones, and more or less tinged with brown; primary and secondary quills blackish-brown, the outer primaries just edged with white; wing coverts and tertiaries of a rather lighter reddish-brown than the back, and marked with oval black spots, most conspicuous on the tertiaries; under wing coverts grayish-plumbeous; bill dark brown, base of under mandible yellowish; feet reddish.

Length (fresh) 12 in.; wing 5⅞; tail 5; bill 1¾; tarsi 1.

Habitat. Socorro Island, Mexico. Collected by Col. A. J. Grayson. Type in Museum Smithsonian Institution, No. 50855.

There is no difference in the plumage of the sexes. Three specimens are in the collection, one of which is rather more olivaceous on the back; otherwise all are alike.

The tail consists of fourteen feathers, as in the two others of the genus; the shape of the tail is like that of *Z. yucatanensis*, the feathers not pointed as in *Z. carolinensis*.

Remarks. It bears no resemblance to *Z. carolinensis;* compared with *Z. yucatanensis*, they are somewhat alike in coloring below, but in *Z. graysoni* the color is more uniform and much darker; it differs from both species in the absence of metallic coloring on the neck.

Note and observations by Col. Grayson.

"*The Solitary Dove.* Iris dark brown; bill dark brown, with a slight tinge of red; base of under mandible reddish-purple, as also the base of the gape; tarsi and toes reddish flesh-color, posterior portion of which is paler, nails brownish-black; bare space extending from base of bill to and around the eye plumbeous; second and third primary quills longest; tail graduated, with fourteen feathers, outer ones $1\frac{1}{2}$ inches shorter than the central. Not abundant.

"Of all the birds I met with in the Island, this seemed to be the most lonely; not a flock or even a pair were ever seen together. They are remarkably tame, perhaps more so than any bird of this order; one was captured by hand as it came into our camp, and perched upon the rude table on which I was at work. Its melancholy look appeared to be in keeping with the solitude of, and its sombre plumage corresponding with the gray brush and brown volcanic rock composing its wild home. In form and appearance, when alive, it resembles the common Turtle Dove.

"The first specimen seen and captured was by my son, Edward Grayson, whose name this evidently new species should bear—not for this discovery alone, but for the assistance often rendered, in making my collections, and more particularly on this expedition, in which he was indefatigable, even to enthusiasm, in aiding its progress, as well as the advancement of science, in the cause of which he came to an untimely death!"

16. Note on *Rallus longirostris*, Boddaert.

I received a specimen of *Rallus* in a collection from Bahia, which I was unable to determine and was inclined to consider undescribed; from the stoutness of its bill, I named it provisionally *R. crassirostris*. In 1868 Messrs. Sclater and Salvin gave a most valuable and complete "Synopsis of the American Rails" (Proc. Zool. Soc., p. 442). Not being able to make it agree satisfactorily with any of the species therein enumerated, and an opportunity offering to send it to them, as they had lately so fully investigated the Rallidæ, I did so.

On returning it, Mr. Sclater wrote, "is true *longirostris*, figured Pl. Enl. 849." I infer from this (although not distinctly so stated) that they consider it different from *crepitans*; the two birds are very unlike, and no one with the two before him could confound them. If right in my inference, this would be a change of opinion since the publication of the Synopsis, wherein *crepitans* is put as a synonym of *longirostris*; this view has also been taken by other recent writers, adopting Mr. Cassin's suggestion of their probable identity.

I find it agrees with Buffon's plate (which is of reduced size) in the apparent color of the back, also in the form and stoutness of the bill; but they differ in the coloring below, which in the plate is more like *crepitans*, being of an ashy-fulvous, instead of uniform light rufous; they differ also in the bars on the flanks. The only characters, then, on which it can assume the name of *longirostris*, are the shape of the bill and the color of the back, if these are deemed sufficient to overrule the coloring below, in which the plate resembles *crepitans*.

My specimen differed so much from *crepitans*, as well as from all others, that I considered it undescribed at the time, taking for a settled fact that *crepitans* and *longirostris* were the same; if the Bahia bird is to take the name of *longirostris*, it being certainly distinct from *crepitans*, the latter name must be restored to full specific rank.

The bird from Bahia is grayish-olive above, flammulated with blackish-brown; the under-plumage is light rufous, the throat white; a stripe of dull rufous extends from over the eye to the bill; the sides and under wing coverts are brown, with transverse narrow white bars; the upper mandible is brown on the ridge and at the end, the remaining part and the lower mandible dark yellow; feet yellow.

Length 12 in.; wing $5\frac{1}{2}$; tail $2\frac{1}{4}$; bill $2\frac{1}{4}$ to rictus; tarsi $1\frac{3}{4}$.

It is smaller in all its measurements than *crepitans*, and has the bill fully twice as deep as in that species, the tarsi are shorter, the feathers of the back are bordered with grayish-olive instead of light bluish-cinereous, and the color below of a clear light rufous instead of an ashy-fulvous; the colors are more like those of *R. elegans*, but are lighter; its smaller size, shorter and stouter bill, distinguishes it also from that species.

The description of *R. longirostris* in Messrs. Sclater and Salvin's Synopsis is evidently taken from United States specimens of *crepitans*. I have seen no description at all applicable to my Bahia specimen, and if the evidence is not considered sufficient for it to assume the name of *longirostris*, it may then bear that of *crassirostris*.

The new species of *Vireo*, described below, is added to my paper by request of Professor Baird. The description and remarks are his, without alteration by me.

Vireosylvia magister, BAIRD, n. s.

Habitat. Belize, Br. Honduras.

Bill stout and lengthened. Wings considerably longer than the nearly even, though rather short and decidedly rounded tail; the 1st quill about equal to the 6th, or very little longer; the 3d longest; the 2d and 4th a little shorter. No spurious primary.

Upper parts olive-green, brightest on rump and tail; the head above, and to a less degree the back, with a slight gloss of ashy, but without forming a cap. Beneath dull olivaceous-white, the belly (and the tibiæ somewhat) rather buffy yellow; the sides of neck and body olivaceous. Axillars and inner wing coverts sulphur yellow; the crissum similarly colored, but duller. Quills almost black, edged internally with grayish-white, externally with olive; tail feathers more olive-brown, edged internally with greenish-yellow, externally with bright olive. A broad stripe of pale yellowish from bill over and behind eye to nape, becoming paler when it reaches the eye, and with a faint indication of a dusky border above it; a dusky brown, well-marked stripe from bill to eye, and a small spot of the same behind it. The bill is almost black, except the basal half of lower mandible, which appears to have been nearly white. The legs are blackish-plumbeous. " Iris brown " (*Wood*)?

Total length, 6.00; wing, 3.00; tail, 2.50; difference between 9th and longest quills, .60; exposed portion of 1st primary, 1.90, of 2d, 2.15, of longest (measured from exposed base of 1st primary), 2.24; length of bill from forehead, .80, from nostril, .46, along gape, .90; tarsus, .83; middle toe and claw, .70, claw alone, .24; hind toe and claw, .56, claw alone, .27.

This interesting new species of *Vireo* is among the largest of the genus, considerably exceeding in size *V. olivacea*, and fully equal to *V. calidris* of Jamaica. In general appearance it closely resembles the latter, but there is even less of the grayish cap, and the dusky mandibular stripe is wanting; the under parts are rather more olivaceous; the bill is of about the same size. The much rounded wings constitute an important character of the species.

The much larger size, almost black bill and feet, absence of ashy cap, more olivaceous under-parts, will readily distinguish the species from *V. olivacea*. The wings, also, are much more rounded; the first quill about equal to the sixth, instead of being but little shorter than the fourth. The wing formula is much the same as that of *V. agilis*, but the size and coloration are very different.

This species is one of several new species of birds in a collection made at Belize, British Honduras, for Dr. Henry Bryant, by Mr. Christopher Wood.

II.—*Notes on the genus* PINERIA, *and on the lingual dentition of* PINERIA VIEQUENSIS, *Pfeiffer*.

BY THOMAS BLAND AND W. G. BINNEY.
Read March 20, 1871.

THE genus *Pineria* was established by Poey in 1854 (*Memorias*, I., 428), and thus characterized:—

T. bulimiformis, imperforata, turrita, apertura rotundata, peristoma simplex, rectum, undique acutum. Animal nudipes tentaculis duobus retractilibus instructum, apice oculatis; labrum rotundatum; reptatio sinuosa.

Poey described two species, *P. terebra* and *Beathiana*, both from the Isle of Pines, of which figures are given (*Memorias*, l. c., tab. 34, f. 12–18).

He remarks that he had examined the living animal of *P. Beathiana* with great care, but could detect no trace of "inferior tentacles," and Dr. Gundlach had satisfied himself of their absence in *P. terebra*. Observing that the form of shell (columella excepted) and sculpture of the former species was somewhat like that of *Macroceramus turricula*, Pfr., Poey studied its soft parts and found such tentacles existing.

In 1856 Pfeiffer (*Malak. Bl.* III. p. 46) described *Bulimus Viequensis*, from Vièque, and suggested its alliance with *Pineria*. The species is figured in *Notit. Conch.* Fasc. xxxi. t. 93, f. 39–41.

The late Rev. H. Parkinson, in 1857, discovered *P. Viequensis* in Barbados.

In 1858 Fischer (*Journ. Conch.* vii. 184, t. 7, f. 7–8) described *Helix Schrammi*, from Guadaloupe.

Pfeiffer (*Mon.* vi. 343) adopts the genus *Pineria*, for *B. Viequensis*, *H. Schrammi*, and Poey's two species, and remarking on the evident affinity of Fischer's species with *Vie-*